Turning The Page Written By Grace

Joshua Rhoades

Published by Joshua Paul Rhoades, 2024.

While every precaution has been taken in the preparation of this book, the publisher assumes no responsibility for errors or omissions, or for damages resulting from the use of the information contained herein.

TURNING THE PAGE WRITTEN BY GRACE

First edition. September 26, 2024.

Copyright © 2024 Joshua Rhoades.

ISBN: 979-8227537591

Written by Joshua Rhoades.

Also by Joshua Rhoades

Courage Under Fire: David's Stand On The Battlefield
Jonah's Journey: Voices Of Redemption And Lessons In Obedience
The Furnace Of Faith: 12 Principles From The Heat Of Faith
Whispers of Hope: Inspiring Stories of Men's Prayers In Scripture
Frontier Legends: The Oregon Dream
Elijah: A Beacon Of Boldness
HOOK, LINE & SAVIOUR - Faith Reflections from Fishing
Driven By Faith: Motor Racing Inspired Christian Life
30 Day Devotional - Bold and Strong- Coffee Devotions for a Courageous
Christian Walk
Authentic Christianity: The Heart of Old Time Religion
Consider The Ant - God's Tiny Preachers
Flee Fornication: The Plea For Purity
Renewed Hope- How to Find Encouragement in God
Sounding The Call - The Voice of Conviction
The Altar - Where Heaven Meets Earth
The Bible's Battlefields- Timeless Lessons from Ancient Wars
The Sacred Art of Silence - How Silence Speaks in Scripture
Under Fire- The Sanctity of the Traditional Biblical Home
Who Is on the Lord's Side? A Call to Righteousness
What Is Truth? - From Skepticism to Submission
First and Goal- Faith and Football Fundamentals
From Dugout to Devotion- Spiritual Lessons from Baseball
Par for the Course- Faith and Fairways
The Believer's Pace- Tools for Running Life's Marathon
The Immutable Fortress- Security in God's Unchanging Nature
Biblical Bravery
Deer Stands and Devotions: A Hunter's Walk with God

Dedication

To you, dear reader, I want to dedicate this book with all my heart. Whether you picked up "Turning The Page – Written By Grace" out of curiosity, or perhaps in search of hope, I want you to know this: you are seen, you are known, and you are loved by the Author of life. No matter where you are right now, no matter what chapter of life you feel stuck in—whether it's one filled with sorrow, pain, loss, or regret—God is not done with your story.

This book is for the broken-hearted, for those who feel like their best days are behind them, for those who feel like they've reached the end of the road. Maybe you've faced a setback so painful that you think your story is finished. Maybe you've experienced a failure so devastating that you believe you're beyond hope or redemption. Or maybe you're simply tired, weary from a season of waiting, uncertainty, and silence.

I dedicate this book to you because I want you to know that God is still writing your story. He is the God who turns pages, even the ones that feel heavy and impossible to move. When you think there's nothing left to say, He speaks life. When you think the story is over, He begins a new chapter. His grace is woven into every part of your life—even the parts that seem broken or messy. He takes the torn and tattered pages of our lives and rewrites them with His love, grace, and purpose.

I pray that as you read this book, you'll feel God's presence gently turning the pages of your life. I hope you'll be encouraged to look at the stories of those in Scripture who felt like their stories were over—Peter, who denied Jesus three times and believed his failure was final; the woman with the issue of blood, who thought her suffering would last forever; Moses, who thought his mistakes had disqualified him from leading. Yet, in every case, God wasn't finished. He restored, redeemed, and rewrote their stories in ways that they could never have imagined.

And He will do the same for you.

God sees every tear you've cried. He knows the weight of every burden you carry. He hears every whispered prayer that you thought went unanswered. And even when you can't see it, He is working. He is turning the pages of your story with grace, writing a narrative that is greater than anything you could have dreamed.

So to you, the reader who may feel unseen, unheard, or forgotten—this book is for you. You are not alone in your struggles, and you are not at the end of your story. With God, there is always another chapter, always hope, always grace to carry you forward. I pray that this book speaks to your heart and reminds you that the best is yet to come. Your story, written by grace, is far from over.

With love and hope for what God will do next in your life,
Joshua Rhoades

Introduction

Have you ever reached a moment in life where you felt like your story was over? Perhaps you found yourself at a dead end—an unexpected loss, a broken relationship, a failure so great that it seemed impossible to recover. In these moments, it's easy to feel like your story is finished, that there's no way forward. But the truth is, God is still writing your story, even when you think the final chapter has already been written.

"Turning the Page – Written by Grace" is a journey through Scripture that reminds us how the Lord is still crafting our lives, even in times of doubt, despair, and defeat. Throughout the Bible, we find countless examples of people who thought their stories were finished, only to discover that God was just beginning a new chapter. From the broken and hopeless to the doubting and fearful, God's grace turned their pages and wrote a story of redemption, hope, and victory. He took lives that seemed shattered and turned them into powerful testimonies of His goodness and grace.

Take a look at Peter, who, after denying Jesus three times, wept bitterly, believing that his failure had disqualified him from being a disciple. In his darkest moment, Peter felt like his story had reached its tragic conclusion. But Jesus, after His resurrection, lovingly restored Peter, giving him a new purpose and calling him to "feed my sheep." Peter's failure wasn't the end of his story—God's grace had written a new chapter, one of leadership and boldness that would change the course of the early Church.

Or consider the woman with the issue of blood, who had suffered for twelve long years. She had spent all her resources seeking a cure, and after years of pain, isolation, and rejection, she must have believed that her life's story would be one of endless suffering. But one encounter with Jesus changed everything. By simply touching the hem of His garment in faith, she was healed, and her story was rewritten by the touch of grace.

And then there's Moses, who thought his story was over after he fled Egypt in fear. A fugitive living in the wilderness for forty years, Moses believed that his chance to lead had been lost. Yet God wasn't done with him. In a burning bush, God called Moses to return to Egypt and lead His people out of slavery, writing a story that would be told for generations to come.

In this book, you'll walk alongside these and many other people from Scripture whose lives were rewritten by God's grace. Their stories remind us that our darkest moments are not the end. The Lord, who is the Author and Finisher of our faith, is still at work. He is turning the page on your story, writing a masterpiece of grace, redemption, and hope. No matter where you find yourself today, know that God is not finished with you yet. Your story, written by grace, is still unfolding, and the best is yet to come. So, take heart and turn the page—there's more to your story than you could ever imagine.

Chapter 1 - The Woman at the Well

The story of the woman at the well in John 4 is a powerful reminder of how Jesus meets us in our brokenness and offers something that can truly satisfy the deepest needs of our hearts—His grace, symbolized as "living water." This account begins with Jesus traveling through Samaria, a place where most Jews would avoid, showing that God doesn't avoid places or people that others might reject. In verse 7, we are told, "There cometh a woman of Samaria to draw water: Jesus saith unto her, Give me to drink." This may seem like an ordinary moment at first, but it quickly becomes a turning point in this woman's life. She had come to the well at a time when others weren't around, perhaps to avoid the judgment of those who knew her story, a story full of brokenness, failed relationships, and likely a deep sense of shame. The well, which provided the water she needed for her daily life, became the place where she would encounter the living water she didn't even realize she was thirsting for. When Jesus asked her for a drink, it wasn't just about quenching His physical thirst. It was about starting a conversation that would reveal the thirst in her own soul—a thirst for acceptance, healing, and hope. The woman, surprised that a Jewish man would even speak to her, let alone ask her for water, responds in confusion, wondering why He, a Jew, would ask her, a Samaritan, for anything. Samaritans and Jews didn't associate with one another, but Jesus wasn't concerned with societal divisions. He wasn't bound by the prejudices of the day. His mission was—and still is—to reach the heart of every person, no matter their background or their past. In verse 10, Jesus responds to her question with a profound statement: "If thou knewest the gift of God, and who it is that saith to thee, Give me to drink; thou wouldest have asked of him, and he would have given thee living water." Here, Jesus begins to reveal who He truly is—the One who offers not just temporary satisfaction, but eternal fulfillment. The woman, still thinking of physical water, is intrigued but doesn't yet understand what He means. She points out that the well is deep, and Jesus has nothing to draw water with. "From whence then hast thou that living water?" she asks in verse 11. Jesus, of course, is speaking of something far greater than the water at the bottom of that well. He's offering a relationship with God, one that quenches the thirst of the soul. In verse 13, Jesus explains, "Whosoever drinketh of this water shall thirst again: But whosoever drinketh of the water that I shall give him shall never thirst; but the water that I shall give him shall be in him a well of water springing up into everlasting life." This is the heart of Jesus' message to her, and to all of us. The things of this world—whether they be relationships, success, or material possessions—will never truly satisfy us. We will always thirst again. But the water Jesus offers, His grace, fills us completely and gives us everlasting life. It's more than just forgiveness of sins—it's a complete transformation of who we are, restoring us to the relationship with God that we were always meant to have. At this point, the woman, still not fully understanding but knowing she wants what Jesus is offering, says in verse 15, "Sir, give me this water, that I thirst not, neither come hither to draw." She is still thinking about avoiding the daily task of drawing water from the well, but her heart is beginning to open. Jesus then shifts the conversation, showing her that He knows the deepest parts of her life, the parts she's tried to keep hidden. In verse 16, He says, "Go, call thy husband, and come hither." The woman replies in verse 17, "I have no husband." Jesus, knowing her story, responds, "Thou hast well said, I have no husband: For thou hast had five husbands; and he whom thou now hast is not thy husband." In this moment, Jesus is not condemning her but rather revealing that He knows her completely—her mistakes, her pain, her shame—and yet, He is still offering her living water. This is the grace of God: knowing us fully, yet loving us completely. The woman, astonished that Jesus knows her life story, begins to realize that this is no ordinary man. She says in verse 19, "Sir, I perceive that thou art a prophet." Jesus, however, takes the conversation even deeper, pointing her toward the true nature of worship and the heart of God's desire for all people. In verse 24, He declares, "God is a Spirit: and they that worship him must worship him in spirit and in truth." Jesus is showing her that true worship is not about the physical location or religious practices; it's about a relationship with God that is genuine and from the heart. This conversation changes everything for the woman. She begins to realize that Jesus is more than just a prophet. She dares to hope that He might even be the Messiah. In verse 25, she says, "I know that Messias cometh, which is called Christ: when he is come, he will tell us all things." Jesus then reveals Himself fully to her, saying in verse 26, "I that speak unto thee am he." This is the turning point. The woman came to the well to get water, but she leaves having met the Savior of the world. Her life, once defined by brokenness and shame, is now transformed by grace. She runs back to the city, telling everyone she meets, "Come, see a man, which told me all things that ever I did: is not this the Christ?" (verse 29). Her testimony brings many others to Jesus, and they too believe, not just because of her words but because they encounter Jesus for themselves. This story of the woman at the well teaches us that no matter how broken we feel, no matter what our past may look like, Jesus meets us right where we are. He offers us living water—His grace—that satisfies the deepest thirst of our souls. He knows everything about us, and yet He still loves us and offers us a new beginning. When God writes your story, it doesn't matter where you've been or what you've done. What matters is that He is the Author, and He can take even the most broken chapters of your life and turn them into something beautiful. Just like the woman at the well, we can go from being defined by our past to being transformed by His grace, and that is when we truly begin to live.

Chapter 2 - The Healing of the Man Born

In John 9:1-7, we find the story of a man who was born blind, and from the moment he entered the world, his life seemed to be marked by darkness and hopelessness. He was condemned to a life where he could not see the beauty around him or enjoy the simple things that others took for granted. Being blind from birth meant that he had never known what it was like to see the light of day, to witness a sunrise, or even to look into the faces of those around him. In the eyes of society, this man was destined to a life of begging, dependence, and isolation, for in that time, people believed that such a condition was often the result of sin—either his own or that of his parents. The disciples even voiced this belief when they asked Jesus, "Master, who did sin, this man, or his parents, that he was born blind?" (John 9:2). To them, it seemed logical that such a tragedy must have been the result of divine punishment. However, Jesus responded with a profound truth that changed the entire narrative: "Neither hath this man sinned, nor his parents: but that the works of God should be made manifest in him" (John 9:3). This statement was a radical shift in thinking. Jesus was telling His disciples, and us, that this man's blindness was not a curse or a consequence of sin. Instead, it was an opportunity for God to display His power and glory. In other words, this man's story wasn't over; God was still writing it, and what seemed like a permanent condition of darkness was about to be transformed into a testimony of God's goodness and power. As the story continues, Jesus, without any hesitation, proceeds to heal the man in a way that was both unconventional and miraculous. He spat on the ground, made clay with the spittle, and anointed the blind man's eyes with the clay. Then He instructed the man to go and wash in the pool of Siloam. Obediently, the man followed Jesus' command, even though he still could not see. Imagine the faith it took for him to do this—he could have questioned why Jesus was using mud or why he needed to wash in a specific pool. But instead, he trusted Jesus' words and acted on them. When he went and washed, something incredible happened. The man who had never seen a single ray of light in his life suddenly could see! His world, once defined by darkness, was now filled with the vibrant colors and images that had been hidden from him for so long. He could see the sky, the faces of people, and the world around him in a way that he had never imagined. This was no small healing—this was a miracle that changed his entire existence. But the story doesn't end there. After the healing, there is a reaction from those around him. His neighbors and those who had seen him begging for years were astonished. They could hardly believe that the man they had known as the blind beggar was now able to see. Some even questioned whether it was the same man, while others asked how this miracle had occurred. The man, still in awe of what had happened, told them plainly, "A man that is called Jesus made clay, and anointed mine eyes, and said unto me, Go to the pool of Siloam, and wash: and I went and washed, and I received sight" (John 9:11). His testimony was simple, but it was powerful because it came from a personal experience of God's power in his life. However, this miracle did not sit well with everyone. The Pharisees, the religious leaders of the day, were upset because the healing had taken place on the Sabbath. They were more concerned with the letter of the law than with the miraculous work of God that had just occurred. They questioned the man and tried to discredit both him and Jesus. Yet, the man stood firm in his testimony, boldly proclaiming what had happened. Despite the pressure from the Pharisees, he declared, "One thing I know, that, whereas I was blind, now I see" (John 9:25). His story had been changed forever, and no amount of skepticism or interrogation could take that away from him. Even when the religious leaders threw him out of the synagogue for standing by his story, the man's faith remained unshaken. What is even more beautiful is that Jesus didn't leave him alone after the healing. Later in the story, Jesus finds the man again, this time not just to heal his physical blindness but to reveal to him the truth of who He is. Jesus asks him, "Dost thou believe on the Son of God?" (John 9:35). The man, eager to know more, replies, "Who is he, Lord, that I might believe on him?" (John 9:36). Jesus then reveals Himself to the man, saying, "Thou hast both seen him, and it is he that talketh with thee" (John 9:37). In that moment, the man's spiritual eyes were opened as well, and he responded in faith, worshiping Jesus. This encounter between Jesus and the man born blind shows us so much about how God works in our lives. First, it reminds us that our circumstances—no matter how difficult or seemingly unchangeable—are not the end of our story. Just as the man's blindness was not the conclusion of his life, but rather an opportunity for God to work, our struggles, pain, and challenges can also be the very places where God shows His glory. Jesus took what seemed like a hopeless situation and turned it into a testimony that has echoed through the ages. Second, this story teaches us about faith and obedience. The man didn't argue with Jesus or question why He used mud or told him to wash in a certain pool. Instead, he simply obeyed. His faith in Jesus' words led to his healing, and in the same way, when we trust God and obey His leading, we open the door for Him to work miracles in our lives. Third, the story of the man born blind reveals the importance of standing firm in our testimony. Even when the Pharisees questioned him and tried to discredit Jesus, the man held on to the truth of what had happened to him. He didn't have all the answers, but he knew one thing for sure: "Whereas I was blind, now I see." In our lives, there may be times when people doubt or challenge our faith, but like the man in this story, we can stand confidently in the truth of what God has done for us. Lastly, this story reminds us that Jesus doesn't just heal us physically or solve our immediate problems—He goes deeper. After the man received his sight, Jesus sought him out again to reveal Himself fully as the Son of God. Jesus didn't just want to heal his eyes; He wanted to heal his heart and give him the gift of eternal life. In the same way, Jesus is not only interested in fixing our external problems—He wants to transform our hearts and bring us into a relationship with Him that goes beyond the physical and into the eternal. When God writes your story, it may not always follow the path you expect. The man born blind probably never imagined that his condition, which seemed like a curse, would become the very thing that led to one of the most powerful encounters with Jesus in the Bible. But God's plans are higher than ours, and He can take even the darkest circumstances and use them for His glory. Whether we are facing physical, emotional, or spiritual challenges, we can trust that God is still writing our story, and like the man born blind, our testimony can be one of God's grace, power, and love. Through this story, we learn that no situation is too difficult for God to redeem, and no person is too far gone for Him to reach. Just as Jesus brought light to a man who had known only darkness, He can bring hope, healing, and transformation to our lives as well. All we need to do is trust Him, obey His word, and believe that He is still at work, writing our story in ways that will bring glory to His name.

Chapter 3 - The Adulterous Woman

In John 8:1-11, we find a story of incredible grace and forgiveness, a story where God steps into a moment of absolute shame and transforms it into an opportunity for redemption. This is the account of the adulterous woman, a woman who had been caught in the act of sin and was brought before Jesus by the religious leaders, the scribes and Pharisees, who were eager to use her situation as a trap to test Him. They dragged her through the streets, likely humiliated and terrified, and threw her at Jesus' feet, declaring that the law of Moses commanded her to be stoned for her sin. In their eyes, her fate was sealed. Her life seemed to be over, her story finished, and the only thing left for her was punishment. But what happens next is one of the most powerful demonstrations of God's mercy in all of Scripture, and it shows us that when God writes your story, even the darkest moments can be redeemed, and no sin is too great for His forgiveness. The religious leaders, full of self-righteousness and eager to test Jesus, asked Him, "Master, this woman was taken in adultery, in the very act. Now Moses in the law commanded us, that such should be stoned: but what sayest thou?" (John 8:4-5). They were trying to trap Jesus, to force Him into a position where He would either have to contradict the law of Moses or show mercy in a way that they could accuse Him of disregarding the law. They didn't care about the woman's life or her future; she was just a pawn in their scheme. But Jesus saw right through their intentions, and instead of responding immediately, He did something unexpected. He stooped down and began writing on the ground with His finger. The Bible doesn't tell us what He wrote, and there has been much speculation about it, but what matters most is that Jesus' response was not what anyone expected. The religious leaders, growing impatient, continued to press Him for an answer. But Jesus, calm and wise, straightened up and said to them, "He that is without sin among you, let him first cast a stone at her" (John 8:7). This simple yet profound statement turned the entire situation upside down. In one sentence, Jesus shifted the focus from the woman's sin to the condition of the hearts of those who were accusing her. His words pierced through their self-righteousness and exposed the hypocrisy in their hearts. One by one, the accusers, starting with the eldest, began to leave, convicted by their own consciences. None of them could claim to be without sin, and therefore, none of them had the right to condemn her. What was supposed to be a moment of condemnation and punishment for the woman became a moment of grace and reflection for her accusers. After they had all left, only Jesus and the woman remained. The contrast between the crowd's judgment and Jesus' mercy could not have been more striking. The woman, who moments earlier had faced what seemed like certain death, now stood before the only one who was truly without sin, the only one who had the authority to judge her. But instead of condemning her, Jesus extended mercy. He asked her, "Woman, where are those thine accusers? hath no man condemned thee?" (John 8:10). She replied, "No man, Lord" (John 8:11). Then Jesus spoke the words that would change her life forever: "Neither do I condemn thee: go, and sin no more" (John 8:11). In this moment, we see the heart of God revealed. Jesus, the sinless Son of God, could have rightfully condemned her. He could have upheld the law and allowed her to be punished for her sin. But instead, He chose to forgive her, to give her a second chance, to write a new chapter in her life. This is the beauty of God's grace—it is not earned, it is not deserved, and it is freely given to those who repent and seek His forgiveness. Jesus did not excuse her sin; He acknowledged it by telling her to go and sin no more. But He did not let her sin define her future. In His eyes, her story wasn't finished, and there was still hope for her to live a transformed life. This encounter between Jesus and the adulterous woman shows us several important truths about how God writes our story. First, it shows us that no one is beyond the reach of God's mercy. This woman was caught in the very act of adultery, and under the law, she was deserving of punishment. But Jesus, full of compassion, did not condemn her. He saw her not just as a sinner, but as a person who was in need of grace. In the same way, no matter what we have done, no matter how far we have strayed, God is always ready to extend His mercy to us. Our sins do not have to be the final word in our story; God's forgiveness can rewrite even the most broken chapters of our lives. Second, this story teaches us about the nature of true justice and mercy. The religious leaders were eager to execute justice according to the law, but their hearts were filled with hypocrisy. They were quick to point out the sins of others while ignoring their own. Jesus' response reminds us that true justice is not about condemning others while overlooking our own faults. Instead, it is about recognizing that we are all in need of God's grace. When we understand our own need for forgiveness, it changes the way we treat others. We are less likely to cast stones and more likely to extend mercy, just as Jesus did. Third, this story is a powerful reminder that Jesus is not finished with us yet. The woman's life could have ended that day with a brutal execution, but Jesus gave her a new beginning. He offered her forgiveness and a chance to turn her life around. In the same way, when we come to Jesus with our sins, our mistakes, and our failures, He doesn't turn us away. He doesn't write us off as hopeless or beyond redemption. Instead, He forgives us, cleanses us, and gives us a fresh start. He says to us, just as He said to the woman, "Go, and sin no more." This doesn't mean that we will be perfect, but it does mean that we are no longer defined by our past. Jesus gives us the power to walk in newness of life, to live a life that is no longer bound by sin but is guided by His grace. Lastly, this story illustrates the difference between the way the world judges and the way God judges. The world is quick to condemn, quick to point fingers, and quick to hold our sins against us. But God's judgment is tempered with mercy. He sees the whole picture—He knows our hearts, our struggles, and our circumstances. And while He does not ignore our sin, He offers us a way out. He offers us forgiveness, redemption, and a new story. When God writes your story, it is not defined by your worst moments. It is defined by His love, His grace, and His ability to bring beauty out of brokenness. The adulterous woman came to Jesus at the lowest point in her life, expecting nothing but condemnation. But what she received was grace, a grace that changed her story forever. Her story was not finished, and neither is yours. No matter what you have done or where you have been, Jesus offers you the same forgiveness and the same opportunity for a new beginning. He doesn't just see you as you are; He sees who you can become through His grace. When God writes your story, it is a story of redemption, a story of second chances, and a story of hope. Just as He did for the adulterous woman, He can take your life, with all its mistakes and failures, and turn it into a testimony of His amazing grace. You may feel like your story is over, like your sin has defined your future, but when you bring your life to Jesus, He writes a new chapter, one filled with mercy, love, and transformation. When God writes your story, the ending is always better than you could have ever imagined, because it is written by the One who knows you fully and loves you completely.

Chapter 4 - The Raising of Lazarus

In the Gospel of John, chapter 11, we read one of the most powerful stories in the Bible, the raising of Lazarus from the dead. This story is a clear example of how, when God writes your story, even death itself does not have the final say. Lazarus, a close friend of Jesus, lived in the town of Bethany with his sisters, Mary and Martha. The three siblings had a close relationship with Jesus, and they were loved by Him. One day, Lazarus fell seriously ill, and his sisters immediately sent word to Jesus, hoping He would come quickly and heal their brother. They believed that Jesus could heal any sickness because they had seen Him perform miracles before. However, instead of rushing to Bethany, Jesus did something surprising—He delayed. When He received the message, He said, "This sickness is not unto death, but for the glory of God, that the Son of God might be glorified thereby" (John 11:4). Jesus knew what was going to happen, and He knew that this situation, which seemed hopeless to Mary, Martha, and everyone else, was actually an opportunity for God's glory to be revealed. Even though Lazarus' condition was worsening, Jesus remained where He was for two more days before setting out for Bethany. By the time Jesus arrived, Lazarus had already been dead for four days. In Jewish tradition, after three days, there was no hope for revival; the body would have begun to decompose, and all hope would have been lost. To the people mourning Lazarus' death, it seemed that Jesus had arrived too late. His story, in their eyes, was finished. When Martha heard that Jesus was coming, she went out to meet Him. Her words expressed both her faith and her sorrow: "Lord, if thou hadst been here, my brother had not died" (John 11:21). Martha believed that if Jesus had come sooner, He could have healed Lazarus. But now, after four days, she believed it was too late. However, even in her grief, Martha's faith in Jesus remained. She said, "But I know, that even now, whatsoever thou wilt ask of God, God will give it thee" (John 11:22). She still believed that Jesus had a special connection with God and that somehow, even in this dark situation, God could still work. Jesus responded with a promise that would challenge and stretch Martha's faith: "Thy brother shall rise again" (John 11:23). Martha, like many Jews at that time, believed in the resurrection of the dead at the end of time. She said, "I know that he shall rise again in the resurrection at the last day" (John 11:24). But Jesus wasn't talking about the distant future—He was about to do something miraculous in the present. Jesus then made one of the most profound declarations in all of Scripture: "I am the resurrection, and the life: he that believeth in me, though he were dead, yet shall he live: And whosoever liveth and believeth in me shall never die" (John 11:25-26). With these words, Jesus revealed His divine power over life and death. He wasn't just a teacher or a prophet—He was the source of life itself. Death, which seemed like the end for Lazarus, was not the final word because Jesus had authority over it. Jesus asked Martha, "Believest thou this?" (John 11:26). And Martha, despite her grief and confusion, responded with faith: "Yea, Lord: I believe that thou art the Christ, the Son of God, which should come into the world" (John 11:27). Even in her sorrow, Martha trusted in who Jesus was, even if she didn't fully understand what He was about to do. After speaking with Martha, Jesus asked to be taken to Lazarus' tomb. By this time, many mourners had gathered to comfort Mary and Martha. When Mary saw Jesus, she also expressed her sorrow, saying, "Lord, if thou hadst been here, my brother had not died" (John 11:32). Her heart was broken, and like Martha, she believed that Jesus could have prevented Lazarus from dying if only He had arrived sooner. Seeing Mary and the others weeping, Jesus was deeply moved. In fact, John 11:35 records the shortest verse in the Bible: "Jesus wept." This verse shows the deep compassion and empathy that Jesus had for His friends. Even though He knew what He was about to do, He was moved by the pain and sorrow of those around Him. Jesus was not indifferent to human suffering—He felt it deeply. But He was also about to show that He had the power to overcome that suffering. When they arrived at the tomb, it was a cave with a stone laid across the entrance. Jesus told them to take away the stone. Martha, ever practical, objected, saying, "Lord, by this time he stinketh: for he hath been dead four days" (John 11:39). To her, opening the tomb seemed unnecessary and even unwise. After all, Lazarus had been dead for four days, and by now, his body would have begun to decay. But Jesus responded, "Said I not unto thee, that, if thou wouldest believe, thou shouldest see the glory of God?" (John 11:40). Jesus was asking for faith, even in the face of what seemed impossible. The stone was rolled away, and Jesus lifted His eyes to heaven and prayed. He thanked God for hearing Him and made it clear that what was about to happen was for the benefit of those standing around, so that they would believe that He was sent by God. Then, in a loud voice, Jesus called out, "Lazarus, come forth" (John 11:43). What happened next was nothing short of miraculous. The man who had been dead for four days walked out of the tomb, still wrapped in the burial cloths. Jesus told them, "Loose him, and let him go" (John 11:44). In that moment, Jesus demonstrated His absolute power over death. Lazarus, whose story seemed to be over, was given a second chance at life. His resurrection was not just a personal miracle for him and his sisters, but a powerful sign to everyone who witnessed it that Jesus truly was the Son of God, the giver of life. This story of Lazarus teaches us several important lessons about when God writes your story. First, it shows us that God's timing is not the same as ours. Mary and Martha wanted Jesus to come right away to heal their brother, but Jesus delayed, not because He didn't care, but because He had a greater plan. Sometimes, when we are in the midst of difficult circumstances, we feel like God is delaying or that He isn't answering our prayers in the way we expect. But this story reminds us that God sees the bigger picture, and His delays are often preparing the way for an even greater miracle. Second, this story teaches us that death does not have the final say. For four days, Lazarus was dead. His family and friends had mourned him, and it seemed that his story was over. But Jesus showed that even death is not beyond His power. In our lives, we may face situations that seem hopeless or beyond repair. We may feel like certain dreams, relationships, or opportunities are dead and gone. But just as Jesus called Lazarus out of the tomb, He can breathe new life into the dead areas of our lives. When God writes your story, no situation is too far gone for Him to redeem. Third, this story reminds us of the importance of faith. Throughout the story, Jesus asked for faith from Martha, Mary, and those around Him. Even when the situation seemed hopeless, He encouraged them to believe that they would see the glory of God. Faith doesn't mean that we always understand what God is doing or why certain things happen, but it does mean trusting that God is in control and that He has the power to bring good out of even the most difficult circumstances. Finally, this story shows us that God's miracles are meant to reveal His glory. Jesus didn't raise Lazarus from the dead just to make Mary and Martha happy, although that was certainly part of it. He did it to reveal who He was—to show that He was the resurrection and the life, and that through Him, all people could have eternal life. When God works in our lives, it is not just for our benefit, but so that others might see His power and be drawn to Him. Lazarus' resurrection was a powerful witness to everyone who saw it, and it led many to believe in Jesus. In conclusion, the raising of Lazarus is a powerful reminder that when God writes your story, He can bring life out of death, hope out of despair, and joy out of sorrow. No matter how hopeless a situation may seem, no matter how long something has been dead, Jesus has the power to bring it back to life. Just as He called Lazarus out of the tomb, He calls each of us to trust Him, to believe in His power, and to let Him write the next chapter of our story. When God writes your story, it is always filled with hope, redemption, and the promise of new life, no matter how dark the circumstances may appear. Just as Lazarus' story wasn't over, neither is yours. When Jesus is involved, even death doesn't have the final say.

Chapter 5 - The Demoniac of Gadara

In Mark 5:1-20, we are introduced to one of the most compelling stories in the Gospels, the story of the demoniac of Gadara. This is a powerful example of what happens when God writes your story, showing that no one is too far gone, no situation is too hopeless, and no darkness is too deep for Jesus to bring deliverance and transformation. This man, who had been possessed by a multitude of demons, lived a life of torment and isolation. He had been driven out of society and lived among the tombs, a place of death and decay. His existence was one of suffering, loneliness, and complete despair. He was beyond the reach of any human help. In fact, the Bible tells us that people had tried to bind him with chains and shackles, but he had broken them apart, and no one could control him. Mark 5:4 says, "Because that he had been often bound with fetters and chains, and the chains had been plucked asunder by him, and the fetters broken in pieces: neither could any man tame him." This man had no peace, no rest, and no hope. Day and night, he wandered among the tombs and in the mountains, crying out in agony and cutting himself with stones. It's hard to imagine a more desperate or tragic situation. He was a man trapped in darkness, both physically and spiritually, and from the outside looking in, it seemed like his story was over, destined to be one of madness and misery until he eventually died. But then, Jesus entered the scene. Jesus and His disciples had crossed the Sea of Galilee and arrived in the country of the Gadarenes, and as soon as Jesus stepped out of the boat, this man came running toward Him. Even though he was controlled by the demons, something in him recognized that Jesus was the only one who could help him, the only one who had the power to break the chains that bound him, not just physically, but spiritually as well. Mark 5:6 says, "But when he saw Jesus afar off, he ran and worshipped him." This moment is so significant because it shows that even the forces of darkness cannot keep someone from coming to Jesus when He calls. The man fell down before Jesus, and the demons within him cried out, "What have I to do with thee, Jesus, thou Son of the most high God? I adjure thee by God, that thou torment me not" (Mark 5:7). The demons recognized Jesus' authority immediately, and they were terrified because they knew that they were no match for the power of the Son of God. Jesus, with His divine authority, commanded the unclean spirit to come out of the man, but before leaving, the demons revealed that they were many. They said, "My name is Legion: for we are many" (Mark 5:9). A Roman legion consisted of thousands of soldiers, so the name Legion indicates that this man was possessed by a vast number of demons, making his situation seem even more hopeless. But even a legion of demons is no match for the power of Jesus. The demons begged Jesus not to send them out of the country, and instead, they requested to be sent into a nearby herd of pigs. Jesus granted their request, and when the demons entered the pigs, the entire herd, about two thousand in number, rushed down a steep hill into the sea and drowned. This dramatic event showed the sheer destructive power of the demons, but it also demonstrated that Jesus had complete control over them. What happens next is one of the most beautiful moments in the story. The man who had been possessed by demons, who had been living among the tombs, cutting himself and crying out in torment, was now completely transformed. Mark 5:15 says, "And they come to Jesus, and see him that was possessed with the devil, and had the legion, sitting, and clothed, and in his right mind: and they were afraid." This man, who had been beyond hope, was now sitting peacefully at the feet of Jesus, fully restored, both physically and mentally. The chains that no human hand could break had been shattered by the power of God. This was a complete and total deliverance. The man's story had been rewritten by Jesus. He was no longer defined by his past, no longer controlled by the demons that had tormented him for so long. His life, which had seemed destined for destruction, was now a testimony of God's power and grace. What makes this story even more powerful is what happens next. The people of the region, when they saw what had happened, were filled with fear. They were afraid of the power that Jesus had demonstrated, and instead of rejoicing over the man's deliverance, they asked Jesus to leave their region. It's tragic that they were more concerned about the loss of their pigs than the miraculous restoration of a man who had been living in torment. But Jesus did not force Himself upon them. He got back into the boat, ready to leave. However, the man who had been delivered begged to go with Him. He had experienced the life-changing power of Jesus, and he didn't want to be separated from the one who had set him free. But Jesus had a different plan for him. Mark 5:19 says, "Howbeit Jesus suffered him not, but saith unto him, Go home to thy friends, and tell them how great things the Lord hath done for thee, and hath had compassion on thee." Jesus sent the man back to his own people to share his story of deliverance. He was no longer the outcast, no longer the man controlled by demons. He was now a living testimony of the compassion and power of Jesus. And that's exactly what he did. Mark 5:20 tells us, "And he departed, and began to publish in Decapolis how great things Jesus had done for him: and all men did marvel." This man's story didn't end with his deliverance—it was just beginning. He became a witness to the transforming power of Jesus, and his testimony caused many people to marvel and to consider the greatness of God. The story of the demoniac of Gadara teaches us several important truths about what happens when God writes your story. First, it shows us that no one is beyond the reach of God's grace. This man was living in the worst possible conditions, controlled by a legion of demons, cut off from society, and beyond the help of any human being. If anyone seemed like a hopeless case, it was him. But Jesus sought him out. Jesus crossed the sea and came to the country of the Gadarenes for this man, showing that God's love reaches even to the most forgotten, the most broken, and the most oppressed. No matter how far gone someone may seem, Jesus has the power to rescue and restore. Second, this story reminds us that Jesus has absolute authority over the forces of darkness. The demons that tormented this man were powerful, but they were powerless before Jesus. They couldn't resist His command, and they had to flee at His word. This is a comforting truth for all of us because it reminds us that no matter what we face—whether it's fear, addiction, oppression, or any other form of bondage—Jesus has the power to set us free. There is no force, no chain, no darkness that can stand against the authority of Christ. Third, this story shows us that Jesus not only delivers us from bondage, but He also restores us to wholeness. When the people saw the man after his deliverance, he was "sitting, and clothed, and in his right mind." Jesus didn't just cast out the demons and leave the man to fend for himself. He brought complete restoration to his mind, his body, and his spirit. This is what happens when Jesus writes your story—He doesn't just take away the bad; He brings healing, peace, and a new beginning. Fourth, the story of the demoniac of Gadara reminds us that our testimony has power. After Jesus delivered the man, He sent him back to his own people to share his story. This man, who had once been feared and rejected, became a witness to the life-changing power of Jesus. And his testimony had an impact. People marveled at what God had done for him. In the same way, when God writes our story, He doesn't just do it for our benefit. He wants to use our story to bring hope and faith to others. Our testimony of deliverance, healing, and transformation can inspire others to believe that Jesus can do the same for them. Lastly, this story reminds us that Jesus sees us as more than our past. This man had been defined by his condition for so long. He was known as the demoniac, the one who lived among the tombs. But Jesus didn't see him as a hopeless case. Jesus saw him as a man in need of deliverance, a man with a future and a purpose. When God writes your story, He doesn't define you by your past mistakes, failures, or struggles. He defines you by His love, His grace, and His purpose for your life. No matter what you've been through, no matter how broken your story may seem, Jesus can rewrite it into something beautiful. In conclusion, the story of the demoniac of Gadara is a powerful example of what happens when God writes your story. It's a story of deliverance, restoration, and transformation. It shows us that no one is beyond hope, no situation is too dark for Jesus to bring light, and no past is too broken for Him to heal. When Jesus steps into your life, He has the power to break every chain, to cast out every fear, and to restore you to wholeness. And just like the man from Gadara, He sends you out to share your story with others, to be a living testimony of His grace and power. When God writes your story, it is a story of hope, of redemption, and of new beginnings. No matter where you've been, no matter how lost you may feel, Jesus is ready to step in, to rewrite your story, and to use it for His glory. Just as He did for the demoniac of Gadara, He can do for you. Your story is not over; it is just beginning when you let Jesus take control.

Chapter 6 - The Paralytic Lowered Through the Roof

In Mark 2:1-12, we find an extraordinary story about a paralyzed man whose life seemed hopeless, his future bound by the limitations of his physical condition. This man could not walk, could not care for himself, and likely relied on others for even the most basic of daily needs. His story was one of helplessness and despair, a life confined by a body that refused to cooperate. No doubt, he had given up hope of ever being healed, resigned to a future that seemed unchangeable, forever dependent on others. But then, something happened that changed everything. Word spread throughout the town of Capernaum that Jesus had returned, and people were excited. They had heard about the miracles He had performed, the lives He had touched, and the power He seemed to carry with Him. Wherever Jesus went, crowds gathered, desperate to catch a glimpse of this teacher who could heal the sick, make the blind see, and give the lame the ability to walk. This paralyzed man had four friends who, despite his situation, had not given up hope. They believed that if they could just get him to Jesus, something miraculous could happen. These friends had faith, not just in the possibility of healing, but in Jesus Himself. They believed that Jesus could do what no one else could do, that He could rewrite their friend's story in a way that no one else could. And so, they decided to take action. When they heard that Jesus was in town, they picked up their friend on his mat and carried him to the house where Jesus was teaching. But when they arrived, the crowd was so large that there was no way to get inside. People were packed into the house, spilling out the doorways, and no one was willing to make room for a paralyzed man on a stretcher. Most people might have given up at that point, but not these friends. Their determination to get their friend to Jesus was stronger than the obstacle before them. They didn't turn back or wait for the crowd to disperse. Instead, they looked for another way. Seeing the flat roof of the house, they decided to do something that no one else had thought of. They climbed up to the roof, carrying their paralyzed friend with them, and then began to tear through the tiles and thatch. It wasn't an easy task, but their faith and determination pushed them forward. They created an opening large enough to lower their friend, on his mat, down into the middle of the room where Jesus was teaching. Imagine the scene: Jesus, surrounded by people, teaching and sharing the Word of God, when suddenly, debris starts to fall from the ceiling. The crowd looks up to see daylight breaking through as a hole opens in the roof. Then, slowly, a man on a mat is lowered right in front of Jesus. The room falls silent. All eyes are on the paralyzed man and the Teacher. Everyone is wondering what Jesus will do. Will He be angry that His teaching has been interrupted? Will He condemn these men for breaking through the roof? But Jesus isn't angry. He sees the determination and faith of the man's friends. He sees their belief that if they could just get to Him, something miraculous could happen. And Jesus, who always responds to faith, does something unexpected. Instead of immediately healing the man's physical condition, He says, "Son, thy sins be forgiven thee" (Mark 2:5). This is remarkable because everyone, including the man, was likely expecting a physical healing. After all, that's why they went to such great lengths to bring him to Jesus—to make him walk again. But Jesus looks deeper. He sees beyond the physical need to the man's spiritual need, and He addresses that first. By saying, "Thy sins be forgiven thee," Jesus is showing that the man's spiritual future is even more important than his physical healing. Jesus is rewriting the man's story not just on the outside, but on the inside. In that moment, Jesus is offering the man the greatest gift of all—the forgiveness of sins. But not everyone in the room is happy with what Jesus says. The scribes, the religious leaders who were there, begin to question in their hearts, "Why doth this man thus speak blasphemies? Who can forgive sins but God only?" (Mark 2:7). They don't understand that Jesus is not just a teacher or a healer—He is the Son of God, with the authority to forgive sins. They are upset because they think Jesus is claiming to do something that only God can do. Jesus, knowing their thoughts, responds with a challenge. He asks them, "Why reason ye these things in your hearts? Whether is it easier to say to the sick of the palsy, Thy sins be forgiven thee; or to say, Arise, and take up thy bed, and walk?" (Mark 2:8-9). In other words, Jesus is asking, what is easier—to heal a man's body or to forgive his sins? Both are impossible for humans, but both are possible for God. Then, to prove that He has the authority to forgive sins, Jesus does what everyone was hoping for. He says to the paralyzed man, "I say unto thee, Arise, and take up thy bed, and go thy way into thine house" (Mark 2:11). Immediately, the man stands up, picks up his mat, and walks out in front of everyone. The crowd is amazed. They have never seen anything like this before. They glorify God, saying, "We never saw it on this fashion" (Mark 2:12). What Jesus does in this moment is more than just a physical healing. He rewrites this man's entire story. A man who had been paralyzed, dependent on others for everything, is now walking, free to live a new life. But more importantly, his sins have been forgiven, and his relationship with God has been restored. Jesus didn't just heal his body; He healed his soul. This story teaches us several important lessons about what happens when God writes your story. First, it shows us the power of faith. The paralyzed man's friends believed that if they could just get him to Jesus, something miraculous could happen. Their faith moved them to take action, even when obstacles stood in their way. They didn't let the crowd or the difficulty of the situation stop them from getting to Jesus. Their determination and faith were rewarded when Jesus not only healed their friend but also forgave his sins. This reminds us that faith is not just about believing with our minds—it's about taking action, stepping out in trust, and doing whatever it takes to bring our needs to Jesus. Second, this story shows us that Jesus cares about more than just our physical needs. The paralyzed man came to Jesus for healing, but Jesus saw that his greatest need wasn't physical—it was spiritual. The man needed forgiveness, and Jesus gave him that first. This reminds us that while our physical needs are important, our spiritual needs are even more so. Jesus wants to heal us from the inside out, to address the deeper issues of our hearts and souls. He cares about our whole being, not just the surface-level problems. Third, this story shows us that nothing is too hard for Jesus. Whether it's healing a paralyzed man or forgiving sins, Jesus has the power to do what no one else can do. The scribes questioned His authority to forgive sins, but Jesus proved that He had both the authority and the power to do the impossible. This reminds us that no matter what situation we find ourselves in, no matter how impossible it may seem, Jesus is able to rewrite our story. He can bring healing, restoration, and forgiveness into even the most hopeless situations. Fourth, this story reminds us of the importance of community. The paralyzed man couldn't get to Jesus on his own. He needed his friends to carry him, to break through the roof, and to lower him down into the room. Without their help, he wouldn't have experienced the miracle of healing and forgiveness. This reminds us that we need each other. Sometimes, we are the ones who need to be carried to Jesus, and other times, we are called to carry others. Faith is not meant to be lived out alone; we need a community of believers to support, encourage, and help us when we can't help ourselves. Lastly, this story shows us that when God writes your story, it is always a story of transformation. The paralyzed man's life was completely changed in that moment. He went from being carried on a mat to walking out of the house on his own two feet. But more than that, his sins were forgiven, and his relationship with God was restored. His physical healing was incredible, but his spiritual healing was even greater. When Jesus steps into our lives, He doesn't just fix the external problems—He goes deeper. He transforms us from the inside out, rewriting our story in ways that we could never imagine. In conclusion, the story of the paralyzed man being lowered through the roof is a powerful example of what happens when God writes your story. It is a story of faith, determination, healing, and forgiveness. It shows us that no obstacle is too great for Jesus, no sin is too big for Him to forgive, and no life is too broken for Him to restore. Just as He did for the paralyzed man, Jesus can rewrite our story, bringing healing to our bodies, restoration to our souls, and hope to our hearts. When we come to Jesus in faith, no matter how impossible our situation may seem, He has the power to do the impossible. When God writes your story, it is always a story of grace, redemption, and transformation.

Chapter 7 - The Widow of Nain's Son

In the story found in Luke 7:11-17, we are given a powerful glimpse into how, when God writes your story, He can take the most hopeless and heartbreaking situations and completely transform them. This is the story of the widow of Nain, whose only son had died, leaving her not only with an overwhelming grief but also with an uncertain and bleak future. In the culture of that time, a widow with no sons had very little hope for survival. She had no one to provide for her, no one to carry on her family name, and no one to comfort her in her old age. This woman's life had been marked by loss—not only had she lost her husband, but now her only son had been taken from her as well. The funeral procession was underway, and the young man's body was being carried out of the city to be buried. For the widow, this must have felt like the end, not only of her son's life but of her own future. In her mind, her story seemed to be over. She was now completely alone, facing a future of uncertainty, poverty, and despair. But just when it seemed like all hope was lost, Jesus entered the scene. In verse 11, we are told that Jesus, along with His disciples and a large crowd, was approaching the town of Nain. As He neared the city gate, He encountered the funeral procession. The body of the widow's son was being carried out, and the widow, surrounded by mourners, was following behind. In that moment, Jesus saw her. The Bible tells us that when He saw her, He had compassion on her. In verse 13, it says, "And when the Lord saw her, he had compassion on her, and said unto her, Weep not." These two words, "Weep not," are so powerful because they show us that Jesus was not indifferent to her pain. He understood the depth of her sorrow and her hopelessness, and He was about to do something that would not only change her life but also reveal His divine power and love. Jesus didn't just see a grieving widow—He saw her broken heart, her crushed spirit, and her uncertain future. And He was moved with compassion. Compassion is more than just feeling sorry for someone; it's a deep, powerful love that drives a person to take action. And that's exactly what Jesus did. He didn't just offer words of comfort—He was about to change her story forever. Without being asked, without any request from the widow or anyone else, Jesus acted out of His own love and compassion. He walked up to the bier, the platform on which the young man's body was being carried, and He touched it. In that moment, everything stopped. The pallbearers stood still, and the crowd must have watched in stunned silence, wondering what Jesus was going to do. No one had ever seen anything like this before. Jesus, the Son of God, was about to do something miraculous. He spoke directly to the lifeless body of the young man and said, "Young man, I say unto thee, Arise" (Luke 7:14). His voice carried authority, an authority that even death itself had to obey. And in that instant, the young man's life was restored. The Bible tells us that "he that was dead sat up, and began to speak" (Luke 7:15). Imagine the shock, the awe, the joy that must have filled that moment. The young man, who had been dead, was now alive again, sitting up and speaking as if he had never left. This was not just a healing—this was a resurrection. Jesus had done the impossible. He had reached into the grip of death and pulled this young man back to life. But the story doesn't end there. After raising the young man from the dead, Jesus did something even more beautiful. He took the young man and delivered him back to his mother. In verse 15, it says, "And he delivered him to his mother." This simple act of returning her son to her was filled with profound meaning. Jesus didn't just give her back her son—He gave her back her hope, her future, and her reason to live. Her life, which had seemed destined for loneliness and despair, was now filled with joy and possibility. The widow's story was rewritten in an instant. What had seemed like the end was now a new beginning. This story teaches us several important truths about what happens when God writes your story. First, it shows us that Jesus sees us in our pain. Just as He saw the widow of Nain in her grief, Jesus sees each of us in our moments of sorrow, loss, and despair. He is not distant or indifferent to our struggles. He is full of compassion, and His heart breaks for those who are hurting. When we feel like no one understands or cares about our pain, we can be assured that Jesus does. He knows every tear we cry, every burden we carry, and He is ready to step into our story with love and compassion. Second, this story reminds us that Jesus has power over even the most hopeless situations. The widow's son was dead. His life was over, and by all human standards, there was no hope of him ever coming back. But Jesus shows us that no situation is beyond His power. Even death, which seems like the ultimate end, must bow to the authority of Jesus. This gives us hope that no matter what we are facing—whether it's a broken relationship, a financial crisis, a devastating loss, or even our own failures—Jesus has the power to bring life and hope into those situations. He can rewrite our story, no matter how dark or hopeless it may seem. Third, this story teaches us about the heart of God. Jesus didn't raise the widow's son just to show off His power or to make a spectacle. He did it out of love. He did it because He cared about the widow and her future. This shows us that God's power is always accompanied by His love. When He steps into our lives, it's not just to fix things or to display His strength—it's because He loves us deeply and wants to restore what has been lost. He wants to give us back our hope, our joy, and our future. Fourth, this story reminds us that when Jesus writes your story, it's never too late for a miracle. The widow's son had been dead, and the funeral procession was already taking place. By all accounts, it was too late. But Jesus shows us that His timing is perfect. Even when it seems like all hope is gone, He can still intervene. He can still bring life where there was death, hope where there was despair, and joy where there was sorrow. His power is not limited by time, and His miracles often come when we least expect them. Finally, this story shows us that when God writes your story, it becomes a testimony to others. After Jesus raised the widow's son, the Bible tells us that "there came a fear on all: and they glorified God, saying, That a great prophet is risen up among us; and, That God hath visited his people" (Luke 7:16). The miracle of the young man's resurrection didn't just impact the widow and her son—it impacted the entire community. People recognized that God had visited them, that something miraculous had happened in their midst. In the same way, when God steps into our lives and rewrites our story, it doesn't just affect us—it becomes a testimony to others. Our story of God's grace, love, and power can inspire faith in those around us. People will see what God has done in our lives, and it will lead them to glorify Him. In conclusion, the story of the widow of Nain's son is a powerful reminder of what happens when God writes your story. It's a story of hope restored, of life given back, and of a future rewritten by the love and power of Jesus. Just as He stepped into the widow's story when all seemed lost, Jesus is ready to step into your story. No matter how hopeless your situation may seem, no matter how much loss or pain you have experienced, Jesus is full of compassion and ready to bring life, healing, and restoration. When He speaks, even death has to bow, and when He writes your story, it is one of redemption and new beginnings. Your story is not over. With Jesus, there is always hope, and there is always a new chapter waiting to be written. When God writes your story, it becomes a testimony of His love and power, a story that not only transforms your life but also brings glory to God and hope to those around you. Just as He gave the widow of Nain her son and her future back, Jesus is ready to give you back what has been lost and to lead you into a future filled with His grace, love, and purpose. When God writes your story, the impossible becomes possible, and the hopeless becomes hopeful. Trust Him with your story, and watch as He does more than you could ever imagine.

Chapter 8 - The Healing of Jairus' Daughter

In the Gospel of Mark, chapter 5, verses 22-43, we find one of the most moving stories of faith, hope, and miraculous healing: the story of Jairus' daughter. This account shows us clearly what happens when God writes your story, reminding us that no matter how final or hopeless a situation may appear, Jesus has the power to rewrite it, even over death itself. Jairus was a ruler of the synagogue, a man of great influence and respect within his community. But even those who hold positions of power and authority are not immune to suffering and pain. Jairus' beloved daughter, just twelve years old, had fallen gravely ill. This young girl, who had her whole life ahead of her, was at the point of death, and Jairus was desperate to save her. He had likely tried everything within his power to help her, but nothing had worked. It seemed that her story was coming to an untimely and tragic end. In his desperation, Jairus turned to Jesus, having heard of the many miracles He had performed. Despite being a respected leader in the synagogue, Jairus didn't hesitate to humble himself before Jesus. He came to Jesus, fell at His feet, and pleaded with Him to come and heal his daughter, saying, "My little daughter lieth at the point of death: I pray thee, come and lay thy hands on her, that she may be healed; and she shall live" (Mark 5:23). This act of faith is significant because it shows that Jairus believed in the healing power of Jesus, even though his situation was dire. He knew that Jesus was his only hope, and so he sought Him out, asking for a miracle. Jesus, moved by Jairus' faith and the urgency of the situation, agreed to go with him. But as they were on their way to Jairus' house, a delay occurred. A woman who had been suffering from a bleeding condition for twelve years touched the hem of Jesus' garment, believing that if she could just touch His clothes, she would be healed. And indeed, she was healed instantly. Jesus, knowing that power had gone out from Him, stopped and took the time to speak with the woman, acknowledging her faith and confirming her healing. This delay, while significant for the woman who had been healed, must have been agonizing for Jairus. Every second counted, and with each moment that passed, his daughter's condition grew worse. The situation seemed more and more hopeless, and then the news came that no parent ever wants to hear. While Jesus was still speaking with the woman, messengers arrived from Jairus' house with devastating news: "Thy daughter is dead: why troublest thou the Master any further?" (Mark 5:35). In that moment, it seemed that all hope was lost. Jairus' daughter had died, and to those who brought the news, it appeared that her story had ended. There was no point, they thought, in bothering Jesus anymore. Death had taken her, and that was the end of it. But Jesus, hearing the news and sensing Jairus' heartbreak and fear, immediately spoke words of reassurance. He said to Jairus, "Be not afraid, only believe" (Mark 5:36). These words were not just a command to trust, but a promise that something miraculous was about to happen. Jesus was telling Jairus that death was not the end of his daughter's story. Jesus, the author of life, had the power to write a new chapter, even in the face of death. They continued on to Jairus' house, and when they arrived, they found a scene of mourning and sorrow. The house was filled with people weeping and wailing, mourning the loss of the young girl. To them, her death was final, and there was nothing left to do but grieve. But when Jesus entered the house, He made a startling statement. He said, "Why make ye this ado, and weep? the damsel is not dead, but sleepeth" (Mark 5:39). To the mourners, this statement must have seemed ridiculous. They knew what death looked like, and they were certain that the girl was gone. In fact, the Bible tells us that they laughed at Jesus, mocking His words because they believed He was out of touch with reality. But Jesus was not out of touch with reality—He was simply in touch with a greater reality, a reality where He held the power over life and death. He saw beyond what the mourners could see, and He knew that the girl's story was not over. Jesus then took control of the situation. He put everyone out of the house except for the girl's parents and His closest disciples—Peter, James, and John. He wanted only those who believed to witness what was about to happen. With the mourners and doubters outside, Jesus went to the room where the girl's body lay. What He did next would change her story forever. Jesus took the young girl by the hand and spoke two simple yet powerful words in Aramaic: "Talitha cumi," which means, "Damsel, I say unto thee, arise" (Mark 5:41). In that moment, something miraculous happened. The girl, who had been lifeless, immediately arose and began to walk. She wasn't just brought back to life in a weak, fragile state—she was fully restored, with strength to stand and walk around. The Bible tells us that her parents were astonished, overcome with amazement at what had just taken place. Their daughter, whom they thought they had lost forever, was alive again, and their sorrow had turned into overwhelming joy. Jesus then instructed them to give the girl something to eat, a simple and practical act that further demonstrated that she was not only alive but fully restored to health. This story is a profound reminder of the power of Jesus to rewrite even the most hopeless of stories. The mourners thought that the girl's story had ended with her death, but Jesus stepped in and changed everything. He showed that death is not the final word when He is involved. When God writes your story, even death must bow to His authority. There are several important lessons we can learn from this story about what happens when God writes your story. First, this story teaches us about the power of faith. Jairus came to Jesus in faith, believing that He could heal his daughter. Even when the situation seemed hopeless, and even when others told him it was too late, Jesus encouraged him to continue believing. "Be not afraid, only believe" are words that we, too, can hold onto in our darkest moments. When all hope seems lost, Jesus calls us to trust Him, to believe that He is able to do the impossible. Faith is not about ignoring reality or pretending that problems don't exist—it's about trusting that God is greater than the reality we see in front of us. Second, this story reminds us that God's timing is perfect, even when it doesn't match our own. Jairus must have been anxious and frustrated when Jesus was delayed by the woman with the issue of blood. Every moment counted for his dying daughter, yet Jesus took the time to stop and heal someone else. From Jairus' perspective, it seemed like a delay, but from God's perspective, it was all part of His plan. Sometimes, in our own lives, it feels like God is delayed, like He isn't moving as quickly as we would like. But just as in this story, God's timing is always perfect, and He is never late. Even when it seems like all hope is gone, He is still able to intervene in ways we could never imagine. Third, this story teaches us that Jesus has authority over life and death. To the mourners, death was the end. They believed that once the girl had died, there was nothing left to be done. But Jesus showed them that He had the power to raise the dead, to bring life out of death, and to rewrite a story that seemed final. This is a powerful reminder that no situation is too far gone for Jesus. No matter how hopeless or dead something may seem—whether it's a dream, a relationship, or even a life—Jesus has the power to bring it back to life. When God writes your story, nothing is impossible. Fourth, this story reminds us that God's ways are often misunderstood by the world. When Jesus said that the girl was not dead but sleeping, the mourners laughed at Him. They didn't understand what He was about to do. In the same way, when God is at work in our lives, there will be times when others don't understand. They may doubt, mock, or even ridicule our faith, but we must hold onto the truth that God's ways are higher than ours. Just because others don't see what God is doing doesn't mean that He isn't at work. We are called to trust Him, even when others don't. Lastly, this story shows us that when God writes your story, it brings hope, restoration, and joy. The young girl's death brought sorrow and despair to her family and community, but when Jesus stepped in, everything changed. What had been a scene of mourning was transformed into a scene of joy and celebration. In the same way, when Jesus steps into our lives, He has the power to turn our mourning into joy. He brings hope where there was once hopelessness, life where there was death, and a future where there seemed to be none. When God writes your story, it is always a story of redemption and restoration. In conclusion, the healing of Jairus' daughter is a powerful testament to the fact that when God writes your story, even the most hopeless situations can be turned around. It is a story of faith, trust, and the miraculous power of Jesus to bring life out of death. Just as He did for Jairus' daughter, Jesus can rewrite our stories, no matter how final or impossible they may seem. Whether we are facing a situation that feels like it is beyond hope or dealing with the loss of something dear to us, we can trust that Jesus has the power to bring restoration and life. When God writes your story, death is not the end—He is the author of life, and He holds the final word. Just as He raised Jairus' daughter from the dead, He can raise the dead places in our lives and give us a future filled with hope, joy, and new beginnings. Be not afraid, only believe, for when God writes your story, it is a story of life, transformation, and victory over every obstacle, even death itself.

Chapter 9 - The Healing of the Woman with the Issue of Blood

In the Gospel of Mark, chapter 5, verses 25-34, we encounter a deeply moving and powerful story about a woman whose life had been marked by suffering and isolation for twelve long years. This woman's story seemed to be one of endless pain, shame, and hopelessness, but when God writes your story, everything can change in a single moment of faith. This particular woman had suffered from an issue of blood, a condition that caused her to bleed continuously for twelve years. In those days, this kind of condition was more than just a physical ailment—it carried with it a heavy social and spiritual burden. According to Jewish law, a woman with a bleeding issue was considered ceremonially unclean, which meant she was not allowed to participate in public worship or interact freely with others. Anyone she touched would also become unclean, and this would force her into a life of isolation and loneliness. She was cut off from her community, from worship, and likely even from her family. Her condition not only caused her great physical discomfort but also deep emotional and spiritual pain. For twelve long years, she had sought help from doctors, spending all that she had on treatments and remedies, but instead of getting better, she only grew worse. Mark 5:26 tells us that "she had suffered many things of many physicians, and had spent all that she had, and was nothing bettered, but rather grew worse." This verse captures the depth of her desperation. She had tried everything humanly possible, sought out every available solution, and exhausted her financial resources, but all of it had failed. Her body was weakened, her spirit likely crushed, and her hope fading away. To everyone around her, it must have seemed that her story was destined to end in disappointment and despair. But then she heard about Jesus. News had spread about this teacher and healer from Nazareth who was performing miracles, healing the sick, casting out demons, and even raising the dead. For this woman, hearing about Jesus must have sparked a small flicker of hope in her heart. After all, if Jesus could heal others, perhaps He could heal her too. Perhaps He could be the one to finally end her suffering. Yet, approaching Jesus would not be easy. She was ceremonially unclean, and being in a crowd risked making others unclean as well. Additionally, she may have felt unworthy to even approach Jesus, given her condition and the stigma attached to it. But despite all these obstacles, her faith was strong enough to drive her forward. She believed that if she could just get close enough to touch His garment, she would be healed. In Mark 5:28, she says to herself, "If I may touch but his clothes, I shall be whole." Her faith was so great that she didn't even feel the need to speak to Jesus or ask Him for healing directly. She believed that simply touching the hem of His garment would be enough. This simple yet profound act of faith shows us that even in her brokenness, she trusted in the power of Jesus to change her life. With that determination, she made her way through the crowd. Imagine the scene: Jesus was surrounded by a multitude of people, all pressing in on Him from every side. But the woman, weak and weary from her years of suffering, pushed through the crowd, unnoticed and anonymous. Her focus was entirely on reaching Jesus. And finally, she did. She reached out her hand and touched the hem of His garment. In that moment, everything changed. Instantly, she felt in her body that she was healed. The bleeding stopped, and for the first time in twelve years, she was free from the pain and suffering that had defined her life. Mark 5:29 tells us, "And straightway the fountain of her blood was dried up; and she felt in her body that she was healed of that plague." It was a miracle, a moment of divine intervention that completely transformed her life. But the story doesn't end there. While the woman may have hoped to slip away quietly, unnoticed by the crowd or by Jesus, something remarkable happened. Jesus, aware that power had gone out from Him, stopped and asked, "Who touched my clothes?" (Mark 5:30). His disciples were confused by the question, given that so many people were pressing against Him, but Jesus knew that this touch was different. It wasn't just a casual brush in the midst of a crowd—it was a deliberate act of faith. The woman, realizing that she could not remain hidden, came forward trembling with fear. She fell at Jesus' feet and told Him the whole truth, confessing her condition, her desperation, and her faith in Him. This moment must have been both terrifying and freeing for her. For so long, she had been defined by her illness and the shame that came with it. But now, standing before Jesus, she was fully known and fully healed. Instead of scolding or shaming her, Jesus responded with words of love, affirmation, and peace. He said to her, "Daughter, thy faith hath made thee whole; go in peace, and be whole of thy plague" (Mark 5:34). In this single sentence, Jesus not only acknowledged her healing but also restored her dignity. By calling her "daughter," He affirmed her identity as a beloved child of God. No longer was she the woman with the issue of blood. No longer was she defined by her illness or her isolation. She was a daughter of the Most High God, healed, restored, and made whole. Jesus' words, "thy faith hath made thee whole," highlight the importance of faith in her healing. It was her faith in Jesus that led her to reach out and touch His garment. Her faith was not in her own strength or in the doctors who had failed her, but in Jesus, the one who had the power to heal her both physically and spiritually. This story teaches us several profound lessons about what happens when God writes your story. First, it shows us that no matter how long we have been suffering, no matter how deep our pain or how hopeless our situation may seem, Jesus is able to heal and restore. This woman had been suffering for twelve years—a long time to endure pain, isolation, and rejection. But in one moment, Jesus completely transformed her life. He did for her what no doctor, no treatment, and no amount of money could do. He healed her. This reminds us that no situation is beyond God's reach. No matter how long we've been struggling, Jesus has the power to step into our lives and change our story. Second, this story shows us the power of faith. The woman believed that if she could just touch Jesus, she would be healed. Her faith wasn't in the garment itself, but in the person wearing it—Jesus. Her faith drove her to push through the crowd, to risk everything just to get close to Him. And her faith was rewarded. Jesus Himself acknowledged that it was her faith that made her whole. This teaches us that when we place our faith in Jesus, when we trust Him with our brokenness and our pain, He is able to do far more than we could ever imagine. Third, this story reminds us that Jesus not only cares about our physical healing, but also about our emotional and spiritual healing. When the woman touched Jesus, she was healed physically, but Jesus didn't let her slip away unnoticed. He stopped and called her out, not to embarrass her, but to restore her fully. By calling her "daughter," Jesus restored her dignity, her identity, and her place in the community. She was no longer an outcast—she was a beloved child of God. This shows us that Jesus is not just concerned with fixing our problems; He wants to make us whole in every area of our lives. He cares about our hearts, our minds, and our souls. Fourth, this story teaches us that when God writes your story, it becomes a testimony to others. The woman's story didn't end with her healing. She came forward and shared the truth about what had happened to her. Her testimony of faith and healing would have inspired those around her, showing them the power of Jesus to transform lives. In the same way, when Jesus heals us, when He steps into our lives and changes our story, it's not just for our benefit—it's so that we can share what He has done with others. Our testimony can encourage and inspire others to believe in the power of Jesus to heal, restore, and redeem. Finally, this story shows us that Jesus sees us. In the midst of a large crowd, with people pressing in on every side, Jesus noticed the touch of one desperate woman. He knew her need, He felt her faith, and He responded to her. This reminds us that Jesus sees each one of us individually. No matter how small or insignificant we may feel, no matter how lost we may seem in the crowd, Jesus knows us. He knows our pain, our struggles, and our faith. And when we reach out to Him, He responds. He doesn't overlook us or dismiss us. He sees us, and He cares deeply about us. In conclusion, the healing of the woman with the issue of blood is a powerful story of faith, healing, and restoration. It shows us that when God writes your story, He can take even the most hopeless and painful situations and turn them into a testimony of His love and power. This woman, who had been suffering for twelve years, who had spent everything she had trying to find a cure, was healed in an instant when she reached out in faith to Jesus. Her life was transformed, her dignity restored, and her faith affirmed. Jesus not only healed her physically, but He also called her "daughter," reminding her—and us—that we are beloved children of God. When Jesus writes your story, it is always a story of healing, restoration, and redemption. No matter how long you have been suffering, no matter how hopeless your situation

may seem, Jesus has the power to step into your life and change everything. Like the woman in this story, all we need to do is reach out to Him in faith, trusting that He is able to heal, restore, and make us whole. And when He does, our story becomes a testimony of His grace and power, a story that can inspire others to believe in the God who writes the best stories of all.

Chapter 10 - The Conversion of Zaccaeus

In Luke 19:1-10, we are told the remarkable story of Zacchaeus, a man whose life was transformed forever by a single encounter with Jesus Christ. Zacchaeus was a wealthy tax collector in the city of Jericho, a position that made him both powerful and deeply disliked by the people. As a tax collector, Zacchaeus worked for the Roman government, collecting taxes from his fellow Jews. But more than that, tax collectors were notorious for being dishonest and greedy, often collecting more than what was required and keeping the excess for themselves. Zacchaeus was no exception; his wealth had come at the expense of others, and because of his position and actions, he was despised by the people around him. He had wealth and power, but he lacked respect, community, and most importantly, he lacked peace. Despite his outward success, Zacchaeus must have known deep down that something was missing in his life. His heart was restless, and though he had gained much material wealth, it had cost him his integrity, his relationships, and perhaps even his self-worth. He was viewed as a traitor, an outcast, someone who had chosen wealth over loyalty to his people. Yet, Zacchaeus' story was far from over, because when God writes your story, even the most despised and broken individuals can experience redemption and transformation. Zacchaeus' story took a dramatic turn one day when he heard that Jesus was passing through Jericho. By this time, Jesus' reputation had spread far and wide—He was known for His teachings, His miracles, and for the way He associated with all kinds of people, including those who were considered sinners and outcasts. Something stirred in Zacchaeus when he heard that Jesus was coming to town. Perhaps he had heard about how Jesus welcomed tax collectors and sinners, or maybe he had heard about the miracles Jesus performed. Whatever it was, Zacchaeus was determined to see Jesus for himself. But there was a problem—Zacchaeus was short in stature, and the crowds that gathered to see Jesus were large. There was no way for him to see over the crowd, and given his status as a tax collector, it's unlikely that anyone would have willingly let him through. Yet, Zacchaeus didn't let his physical limitations or the disapproval of the crowd stop him. His desire to see Jesus was stronger than his pride, and so he ran ahead of the crowd and climbed up into a sycamore tree. From this vantage point, he could get a clear view of Jesus as He passed by. This act of climbing a tree was highly unusual for a man of Zacchaeus' wealth and status. It was something a child might do, not a wealthy, grown man. But Zacchaeus was willing to set aside his dignity and climb the tree because he was desperate to catch a glimpse of Jesus. Little did he know that Jesus had already noticed him. As Jesus walked by, He looked up into the tree and called Zacchaeus by name, saying, "Zacchaeus, make haste, and come down; for to day I must abide at thy house" (Luke 19:5). Imagine the shock and wonder Zacchaeus must have felt in that moment. Not only had Jesus noticed him in the tree, but He called him by name and expressed a desire to stay at his house. This was an incredible honor, especially for someone like Zacchaeus, who was considered a sinner and an outcast. In that instant, Zacchaeus realized that Jesus saw him, not just as a wealthy tax collector or as someone despised by others, but as a person in need of redemption. Jesus had come to seek and to save the lost, and that included Zacchaeus. Overwhelmed with joy and excitement, Zacchaeus hurried down from the tree and welcomed Jesus into his home. But not everyone was happy about this. The crowd, upon seeing that Jesus had chosen to stay with Zacchaeus, began to murmur and complain, saying, "That he was gone to be guest with a man that is a sinner" (Luke 19:7). To them, Zacchaeus was unworthy of such an honor. He was a sinner, a man whose wealth had been gained through dishonest means, and they couldn't understand why Jesus would associate with him. But Jesus didn't see Zacchaeus the way the crowd did. Jesus saw beyond Zacchaeus' past, beyond his reputation, and beyond his mistakes. Jesus saw Zacchaeus' potential for repentance and transformation. He saw a man who was lost, but who could be found; a man who was broken, but who could be restored. And that is exactly what happened. As Jesus spent time with Zacchaeus, something incredible took place in Zacchaeus' heart. He experienced a deep sense of conviction and repentance. He realized the wrong he had done and the pain he had caused others. He didn't just feel sorry for his actions—he was moved to make things right. In a remarkable act of repentance and restitution, Zacchaeus stood up and declared, "Behold, Lord, the half of my goods I give to the poor; and if I have taken any thing from any man by false accusation, I restore him fourfold" (Luke 19:8). This was a bold and generous response. Zacchaeus wasn't just offering to return what he had taken—he was offering to repay it four times over. His willingness to give half of his wealth to the poor and to make restitution for his wrongs showed the sincerity of his repentance and the radical transformation that had taken place in his heart. Zacchaeus had encountered the love and grace of Jesus, and it changed him completely. He no longer cared about holding onto his wealth or maintaining his status. His priorities had shifted, and his heart was now aligned with the values of the Kingdom of God—justice, generosity, and humility. Jesus, seeing the genuine change in Zacchaeus, responded with a powerful declaration: "This day is salvation come to this house, forsomuch as he also is a son of Abraham" (Luke 19:9). In this moment, Jesus affirmed that Zacchaeus' repentance and faith had brought about his salvation. He was no longer defined by his past, his greed, or his position as a tax collector. He was now a child of God, a true son of Abraham, not because of his lineage, but because of his faith. Jesus had rewritten Zacchaeus' story from one of greed and dishonesty to one of redemption and restoration. The final verse of this passage encapsulates the heart of Jesus' mission on earth: "For the Son of man is come to seek and to save that which was lost" (Luke 19:10). This is what Jesus came to do, and this is what He did for Zacchaeus. Zacchaeus was lost—lost in his greed, lost in his pursuit of wealth, and lost in the eyes of his community. But Jesus sought him out, called him by name, and brought him back into the fold. Zacchaeus' story, which had once been one of sin and separation from God, became a story of redemption, forgiveness, and transformation. This story of Zacchaeus teaches us several important lessons about what happens when God writes your story. First, it shows us that no one is beyond the reach of God's grace. Zacchaeus was a tax collector, a man who had gained wealth through dishonest means and who was despised by his community. In the eyes of many, he was beyond redemption. But Jesus doesn't see people the way the world sees them. Jesus saw Zacchaeus not as a hopeless case, but as someone in need of salvation. No matter who we are, what we've done, or how far we've strayed, Jesus is always ready to extend His grace to us. Our past mistakes do not disqualify us from receiving God's love and forgiveness. Second, this story reminds us that Jesus seeks out the lost. Zacchaeus didn't expect Jesus to notice him, let alone invite Himself into his home. But Jesus actively sought

Zacchaeus, calling him by name and offering him the opportunity for a new beginning. This is a powerful reminder that Jesus is always seeking those who are lost. He doesn't wait for us to clean up our lives or become worthy of His love. He meets us right where we are, just as He met Zacchaeus up in that sycamore tree. Third, Zacchaeus' story shows us the power of repentance. When Zacchaeus encountered Jesus, he didn't just feel guilty about his past—he took action. His repentance was genuine and was demonstrated through his willingness to make things right. He gave half of his wealth to the poor and repaid those he had wronged four times over. True repentance is not just about feeling sorry for our sins—it's about turning away from those sins and making a real change in our lives. Zacchaeus' repentance was a sign of the deep transformation that had taken place in his heart. Fourth, this story teaches us that Jesus brings salvation and restoration. Jesus declared that salvation had come to Zacchaeus' house, and with that declaration, Zacchaeus was restored to his rightful place as a son of Abraham, a child of God. His story was no longer defined by his sin or by what others thought of him. Instead, his story was now defined by the grace and love of Jesus. When we encounter Jesus, He doesn't just forgive us—He restores us. He gives us a new identity as children of God, and He rewrites our story from one of sin and brokenness to one of redemption and new life. Lastly, Zacchaeus' story reminds us that when God writes your story, it is never too late for change. Zacchaeus had spent years accumulating wealth through dishonest means, and by the time he encountered Jesus, he was a man of considerable status and wealth. But it wasn't too late for him to change. In a single moment, his life was transformed by Jesus' love and grace. No matter how long we have been living in sin, no matter how far we have wandered, it is never too late for God to rewrite our story. In conclusion, the conversion of Zacchaeus is a powerful reminder of what happens when God writes your story. It is a story of grace, repentance, and transformation. Zacchaeus, a man who had been lost in greed and dishonesty, was found by Jesus and given a new life. His encounter with Jesus changed everything—his priorities, his actions, and his heart. When Jesus writes your story, it is a story of redemption, a story where even the most despised and broken individuals can experience the love and grace of God. No one is beyond the reach of Jesus, and no situation is too far gone for Him to redeem. Just as He called Zacchaeus by name and brought salvation to his house, Jesus is calling each of us by name, offering us the chance to have our story rewritten by His grace. When God writes your story, it is a story of new beginnings, of restoration, and of salvation. Like Zacchaeus, we are invited to come down from our tree, to welcome Jesus into our lives, and to experience the incredible transformation that only He can bring.

Chapter 11 - The Calling of Matthew

In Matthew 9:9-13, we witness a life-transforming moment that shows the incredible power of Jesus to change anyone's story. It's the story of Matthew, also known as Levi, a tax collector whose past was filled with dishonor, greed, and a tarnished reputation. Matthew's job as a tax collector placed him in a despised class of people, especially among his fellow Jews. During the time of Jesus, tax collectors were considered traitors because they worked for the Roman government, collecting taxes from their own people to fund the occupying Roman forces. To make matters worse, tax collectors often overcharged and kept the extra for themselves, becoming wealthy at the expense of others. Matthew, like most tax collectors, would have been seen as someone who had sold out his people for personal gain, putting his love of money above loyalty to his community and faith. He would have been shunned by the religious leaders and most of the people around him, viewed as a sinner unworthy of respect or redemption. Despite his wealth, Matthew likely lived a lonely life, isolated by the choices he had made, with few real friends and little hope for his future beyond the riches he had gained through dishonesty. But as we see in this passage, when God writes your story, everything can change, no matter how dark or tarnished your past may be. One day, as Jesus was walking along, He passed by Matthew's tax booth, where Matthew sat collecting taxes as he did every day. What happened next is extraordinary, because instead of avoiding Matthew or condemning him as many others would have done, Jesus looked directly at him and saw more than just a tax collector. Jesus saw a man with a future, a man who could be transformed, a man who was called to be His disciple. In Matthew 9:9, it says, "And as Jesus passed forth from thence, he saw a man, named Matthew, sitting at the receipt of custom: and he saith unto him, Follow me. And he arose, and followed him." With these simple words, "Follow me," Jesus extended an invitation that would forever change Matthew's life. Jesus didn't give Matthew a lecture on his sins or demand that he make restitution before being worthy of following Him. Instead, He simply called Matthew to follow Him, offering grace and redemption in place of judgment and condemnation. This is a beautiful picture of the heart of God, who calls us not because we are worthy, but because He loves us and desires to rewrite our story. The fact that Jesus chose Matthew, a tax collector, to be one of His disciples would have shocked the people of that time. Tax collectors were considered some of the worst sinners, and the idea that a man like Matthew could be called to follow a holy teacher like Jesus would have been unthinkable to many. But Jesus doesn't see people the way the world sees them. Where others saw a sinner and a traitor, Jesus saw someone with the potential to be a disciple, a leader, and a writer of one of the Gospels. Matthew's immediate response to Jesus' call is equally remarkable. There is no record of hesitation, no indication that Matthew questioned whether he was worthy of such a calling, or whether he should give up his profitable career. Instead, the Bible tells us that Matthew "arose, and followed him." In that moment, Matthew left behind his tax booth, his wealth, and the life he had known in order to follow Jesus. It was an act of faith, a response to the grace that Jesus had extended to him. This moment teaches us that when Jesus calls us, He calls us to leave our old life behind. Matthew could have clung to his wealth and his position, but he recognized that the opportunity to follow Jesus was worth far more than anything he had gained through his former life. His decision to follow Jesus was the first step in a new chapter of his story, a chapter filled with purpose, redemption, and transformation. After calling Matthew, Jesus didn't distance Himself from other sinners. Instead, He embraced them, showing that His mission was to reach the lost, the broken, and the outcast. In fact, shortly after calling Matthew, Jesus went to Matthew's house and ate with many other tax collectors and sinners. Matthew, in his newfound joy and freedom, hosted a meal, inviting Jesus and his fellow tax collectors, giving them the chance to meet the one who had changed his life. But this act of kindness and inclusiveness drew criticism from the religious leaders. In Matthew 9:11, the Pharisees, who prided themselves on their outward displays of righteousness and separation from sinners, saw Jesus eating with tax collectors and sinners and asked His disciples, "Why eateth your Master with publicans and sinners?" In their eyes, associating with sinners made a person unclean, and they could not understand why Jesus, who claimed to be a teacher and holy man, would lower Himself to eat with people like Matthew and his friends. But Jesus' response revealed His heart and His mission. He said to them, "They that be whole need not a physician, but they that are sick. But go ye and learn what that meaneth, I will have mercy, and not sacrifice: for I am not come to call the righteous, but sinners to repentance" (Matthew 9:12-13). In this statement, Jesus made it clear that He had not come to spend time with those who thought they had everything together, but with those who were broken, those who were aware of their need for mercy, and those who were lost in sin. Jesus likened Himself to a doctor who comes to heal the sick, not those who think they are already healthy. This is the essence of the Gospel—that Jesus came to seek and save the lost, to bring healing to those who are spiritually sick, and to offer redemption to those who are trapped in sin. Matthew's story is a perfect example of this truth. He was a man who had made choices that led him down a path of sin and isolation, but Jesus sought him out, called him by name, and gave him a new purpose. Matthew's response to Jesus' call shows us that no matter what our past may look like, no matter how far we've fallen or how unworthy we may feel, Jesus offers us a new beginning. When God writes your story, He doesn't focus on your past mistakes—He focuses on the future He has planned for you. And that future is one of grace, purpose, and transformation. After becoming a disciple, Matthew's story didn't end with just following Jesus. He went on to become one of the twelve apostles, and even more significantly, he was inspired by the Holy Spirit to write the Gospel of Matthew, one of the four Gospels in the New Testament. This Gospel has been read by millions of people throughout history, sharing the life, teachings, and miracles of Jesus Christ with the world. It's incredible to think that a man who had once been a despised tax collector, known for his greed and dishonesty, was chosen by God to write part of the very Word of God. This shows us that when God writes your story, He can use you in ways that you never thought possible. He can take the broken, the rejected, and the sinful and turn them into vessels of His grace and truth. Matthew's transformation from tax collector to apostle and Gospel writer reminds us that no one is too far gone for God to use. God specializes in taking the least likely people and turning their lives into testimonies of His power and love. Just as He did with Matthew, God can take our lives, no matter how messy or broken they may seem, and turn them into something beautiful. The calling of Matthew also teaches us about the power of grace. Matthew didn't earn his way into discipleship through good works or by cleaning up his life first. He didn't have to prove himself worthy before Jesus called him. Instead, Jesus extended grace to Matthew right where he was, and it was that grace that changed him. In the same way, God's grace is available to all of us, not because we deserve it, but because of His love for us. Grace is the foundation of Matthew's story and the foundation of our own stories when we choose to follow Jesus. Furthermore, Matthew's willingness to leave everything behind to follow Jesus challenges us to examine our own lives. Are we willing to let go of the things that hold us back from fully following Jesus? For Matthew, it was wealth, status, and a way of life that had brought him comfort but had also trapped him in sin. For us, it may be different things—material possessions, unhealthy relationships, pride, fear, or sin. Whatever it is, Jesus calls us to let go of the things that keep us from fully embracing His call. When we do, we find that the life He offers is far greater than anything we could leave behind. Matthew's story also reminds us of the importance of humility. Despite his past, Matthew didn't let pride keep him from answering Jesus' call. He didn't make excuses or try to justify his actions—he simply responded with obedience. Humility is essential when it comes to following Jesus. It requires us to acknowledge our need for Him, to recognize that we can't save ourselves, and to accept His grace with open hands. When we humble ourselves before God, He lifts us up, just as He did with Matthew. In conclusion, the calling of Matthew is a powerful reminder that when God writes your story, He can transform even the most unlikely person into a vessel of His grace and truth. Matthew, a tax collector with a tarnished reputation, was chosen by Jesus to be a disciple, despite his past. Jesus didn't see Matthew for who he had been—He saw him for who he could become. And that's how Jesus sees each of us. He looks beyond our mistakes, our failures, and our sins, and He calls us to follow Him into a new life, a life filled with purpose, grace, and transformation. Matthew's story teaches us that no one is beyond redemption, that God's grace is available to all, and that when we respond to Jesus' call, He can use us in ways we never imagined. Just as Matthew went on to become an apostle and the writer of one of the Gospels, we too can be used by God to make an impact in the world when we surrender our lives to Him. When God writes your story, it becomes a story of grace, redemption, and transformation, and it is a story that can change not only your life but the lives of those around you. Just as Matthew's Gospel continues to touch hearts and change lives today, our story, when written by God, can be a testimony of His love and power that impacts the world for His glory.

Chapter 12 - Peter's Restoration After Denial

In the Gospel of John, chapter 21, verses 15-19, we witness one of the most powerful and moving moments of restoration in the Bible, when Jesus, after His resurrection, restores Peter following his devastating denial of Him. This story shows us the immense grace and love of God, and how, when God writes your story, He can redeem even the darkest moments of failure and transform them into opportunities for growth, forgiveness, and renewed purpose. Peter's journey with Jesus had been marked by boldness, enthusiasm, and an unshakable desire to follow Christ. He was one of the first disciples called by Jesus, and he had walked closely with Him for three years, witnessing His miracles, hearing His teachings, and developing a deep bond of friendship and loyalty. Peter was known for his passion and his willingness to speak up, often being the first to declare his faith and allegiance to Jesus. In Matthew 16:16, Peter boldly confessed, "Thou art the Christ, the Son of the living God," and Jesus affirmed Peter's role in the future of the Church by saying, "Thou art Peter, and upon this rock I will build my church" (Matthew 16:18). It was a moment that solidified Peter's identity as a leader among the disciples. But as much as Peter loved Jesus, he was still human, prone to fear, doubt, and failure, just like the rest of us. During the events leading up to Jesus' crucifixion, Peter faced a situation that would test his faith in a profound way. Despite his earlier declaration that he would never abandon Jesus, Peter found himself in the courtyard of the high priest on the night of Jesus' arrest, surrounded by people who recognized him as one of Jesus' disciples. In a moment of fear and weakness, Peter denied knowing Jesus not once, but three times. Each time, his denial became more emphatic, culminating in him swearing, "I know not the man" (Matthew 26:74). Immediately after the third denial, a rooster crowed, just as Jesus had predicted, and Peter's heart broke. Realizing what he had done, Peter wept bitterly, feeling the full weight of his failure. He had denied the very person he loved most, and in that moment, it must have seemed as though his story as a disciple was over. Peter's denial was more than just a personal failure—it was a public betrayal of the one he had pledged to follow unto death. The guilt and shame that Peter carried from that moment must have been overwhelming. After Jesus was crucified and buried, Peter's hopes were crushed. Even after the resurrection, when Jesus appeared to the disciples, Peter likely still wrestled with the memory of his denial and the question of whether he could ever be restored to his former position of leadership. Could Jesus ever trust him again? Could he still have a future in the ministry of the gospel after such a devastating failure? But as we see in John 21, when God writes your story, even your worst failures can be redeemed. The scene is set by the Sea of Galilee, where Peter and several of the other disciples had gone fishing. After a long night of catching nothing, Jesus appeared on the shore, though at first they didn't recognize Him. He instructed them to cast their net on the other side of the boat, and when they did, they caught so many fish that they couldn't haul in the net. It was at this moment that John, the disciple whom Jesus loved, recognized that it was the Lord. Peter, in his typical fashion, jumped into the water and swam to shore, eager to be near Jesus. After sharing breakfast with His disciples, Jesus turned His attention to Peter. In what must have been a heart-pounding moment for Peter, Jesus asked him a question: "Simon, son of Jonas, lovest thou me more than these?" (John 21:15). Jesus didn't address Peter as "Peter," the name He had given him when He called him to be a disciple. Instead, He used Peter's original name, Simon, perhaps signaling that this was a moment of deep reflection and restoration. Jesus was not condemning Peter for his failure; He was inviting Peter into a conversation that would heal the wounds of his denial. Peter responded, "Yea, Lord; thou knowest that I love thee." Jesus then said to him, "Feed my lambs." Jesus was giving Peter a new commission, a task that reaffirmed Peter's role in the kingdom of God. But Jesus didn't stop there. He asked Peter the same question two more times: "Simon, son of Jonas, lovest thou me?" Each time, Peter responded with a heartfelt "Yea, Lord; thou knowest that I love thee," and each time, Jesus gave Peter the command to care for His flock, saying, "Feed my sheep." By asking Peter the same question three times, Jesus was intentionally mirroring the three times that Peter had denied Him. This was not to shame Peter or rub salt in the wound, but rather to offer Peter the opportunity to reaffirm his love and devotion to Jesus. It was a moment of complete restoration. Each of Peter's denials was being replaced with an expression of love and commitment. Jesus was rewriting Peter's story, showing him that his failure was not the end, but rather the beginning of a new chapter in his life. Peter had been forgiven, restored, and entrusted once again with the responsibility of shepherding the people of God. This restoration was not just about Peter's personal relationship with Jesus—it was also about his calling and his future leadership in the Church. Jesus' command to "feed my sheep" was a clear indication that Peter was being called to lead and care for the believers who would come to faith after Jesus' ascension. Despite Peter's failure, Jesus had not given up on him. In fact, Jesus was entrusting Peter with one of the most important roles in the early Church. Peter, the one who had denied knowing Jesus in a moment of fear, was now being called to lead and guide the flock of God with love, humility, and strength. This moment of restoration not only brought healing to Peter's heart, but it also set the course for his future ministry. Peter would go on to become one of the key leaders of the early Church, boldly preaching the gospel at Pentecost, performing miracles in Jesus' name, and ultimately becoming a martyr for his faith. Peter's story is a powerful reminder that when God writes your story, failure is never the end. Even in our lowest moments, when we feel unworthy of God's love and forgiveness, Jesus offers us the chance to be restored, to be made whole, and to step back into the purpose He has for our lives. Peter's denial could have defined him for the rest of his life, but Jesus refused to let that happen. Instead, Jesus gave Peter a new identity and a renewed sense of purpose. He reminded Peter that his love for Jesus was more important than his failure, and that his calling as a disciple and leader was still intact. This story teaches us several important lessons about God's grace and redemption. First, it shows us that no failure is too great for God to forgive. Peter's denial of Jesus was a serious and public betrayal, but Jesus forgave him completely and restored him fully. In the same way, no matter how badly we may have failed, God's grace is always greater. He is always willing to forgive us when we come to Him in repentance, and He is always ready to restore us to our rightful place as His children. Second, this story reminds us that restoration is often a process. Jesus didn't just restore Peter with a single statement—He asked him three times, giving Peter the opportunity to fully confront his failure and receive healing. Sometimes, our restoration takes time, as we work through the pain and guilt of our mistakes. But Jesus is patient with us, walking with us through the process of healing and renewal. Third, Peter's restoration shows us that God's calling on our lives is not revoked because of our failures. Jesus had called Peter to be a leader in the Church, and that calling remained, even after Peter's denial. Jesus' command to "feed my sheep" was a reaffirmation of Peter's calling, reminding him that his purpose had not changed. When we fail, it's easy to believe that we are no longer worthy of the calling God has placed on our lives. But Peter's story shows us that God's plans for us are not canceled because of our mistakes. He is able to redeem and restore us, allowing us to continue walking in the purpose He has for us. Finally, Peter's story teaches us about the importance of love in our relationship with God. Jesus' question to Peter, "Lovest thou me?" gets to the heart of what it means to follow Christ. Our relationship with God is not based on our performance or our ability to never fail—it is based on our love for Him. When we love Jesus, even when we fail, He is there to restore us and to remind us of the depth of His love for us. It is love that motivates us to follow Him, to serve Him, and to fulfill the calling He has placed on our lives. In conclusion, Peter's restoration after his denial of Jesus is a beautiful story of grace, forgiveness, and redemption. It shows us that when God writes your story, failure is not the end—it is an opportunity for growth, healing, and renewed purpose. Peter, who had once denied Jesus in fear, was restored by Jesus and given a new commission to lead and care for the Church. His story reminds us that no matter how far we fall, Jesus is always there to lift us back up, to forgive us, and to restore us to the purpose He has for our lives. When God writes your story, it is a story of love, grace, and redemption, and it is a story that can inspire others to trust in the unfailing love of Christ. Peter's story is a powerful example of how God can take our failures and turn them into opportunities for growth, transformation, and leadership. Just as Jesus restored Peter, He can restore each of us, rewriting our story from one of failure and regret to one of hope and purpose. When God writes your story, no failure is final, and no mistake is beyond the reach of His grace.

Conclusion

As you close the pages of "Turning the Page – Written by Grace", remember this one powerful truth: your story isn't over. No matter where you find yourself—whether in the midst of failure, uncertainty, pain, or even triumph—God is still writing your story. Just as He did with the people in Scripture, He is using every moment of your life to weave a story of grace, redemption, and hope.

Throughout this book, we've journeyed through the lives of individuals who thought their stories had reached a dead end. Peter believed his denial of Jesus had erased his purpose. The woman with the issue of blood thought her suffering defined her future. Moses thought his past mistakes disqualified him from God's plan. But in every case, the Lord stepped in and turned the page. He didn't let their failures or hardships be the final chapter. Instead, He rewrote their lives with grace, giving them new hope and fresh purpose.

The same God who transformed their stories is at work in yours. You may be facing a chapter of uncertainty, hardship, or even loss, but this isn't where your story ends. The Author of your life is still holding the pen, and He is writing a narrative far more beautiful than you could ever imagine. His grace is powerful enough to turn the darkest pages into chapters of victory and transformation.

Now that you've read the stories of Scripture and reflected on the lives of those who have gone before, here's the challenge: trust the Author. Surrender your story to the One who writes with grace, believing that no matter what you've been through or what lies ahead, God is crafting something incredible in your life. When doubt creeps in, when the future feels uncertain, or when you feel like giving up, remember that God never abandons His work. He finishes what He starts.

Ask yourself: How can I embrace the truth that God is still writing my story? What steps of faith can I take, knowing that He's leading me to a greater purpose?

Like Peter, step forward despite past failures. Like the woman with the issue of blood, press through the obstacles in faith, reaching out for Jesus. Like Moses, don't let past mistakes keep you from answering the call of God today.

Moving forward, allow the lessons from this book to fuel your faith and stir your heart. When you feel like your story is at a standstill, remember the stories you've read—of people whose lives seemed to hit rock bottom but who experienced God's grace rewriting their endings. Take courage, because the same God who turned their pages is turning yours.

So, let this be the beginning of your next chapter. Step into it with confidence, knowing that your story is being written by the God who sees every detail, knows every need, and fills every page with grace. Your story, written by grace, is far from over. Keep trusting, keep walking, and keep turning the page, because the best is yet to come.

Don't miss out!

Visit the website below and you can sign up to receive emails whenever Joshua Rhoades publishes a new book. There's no charge and no obligation.

https://books2read.com/r/B-A-AJLBB-FHWAF

BOOKS 2 READ

Connecting independent readers to independent writers.

Did you love *Turning The Page Written By Grace*? Then you should read *Anchored In Truth Exploring The Depths of Psalm 119*[1] by Joshua Rhoades!

[2]

"Anchored in Truth: Exploring the Depths of Psalm 119" is an invitation to dive into one of the Bible's most profound passages, offering a deep exploration of faith, devotion, and the transformative power of God's Word. As the longest chapter in the Bible, Psalm 119 is a masterpiece of spiritual expression, structured as an intricate acrostic with each section beginning with a letter of the Hebrew alphabet. This psalm is not just a collection of verses; it is a meditation on the beauty and necessity of God's law. Through its 176 verses, the psalmist reveals a fervent love for God's commandments, a deep dependence on His guidance, and an unyielding pursuit of understanding and wisdom found only in the Scriptures.

"Anchored in Truth" invites you to explore the rich themes of Psalm 119, offering insights into how God's Word can shape, guide, and sustain a life of faith. This book is crafted not just to help you understand the words of this ancient psalm but to experience them in a way that profoundly impacts your daily walk with God. As you journey through each section, you will see how the psalmist's experiences resonate with the challenges and triumphs of your own spiritual life—whether it's seeking deliverance in trials, finding delight in God's statutes, or pleading for divine guidance.

This book is more than an intellectual study; it is a call to transformation. Psalm 119 urges us to anchor our lives in the unchanging truth of God's Word,

---

1. https://books2read.com/u/mvPayX

2. https://books2read.com/u/mvPayX

making it the foundation of our character, decisions, and ultimate hope. The psalmist's devotion to God's law reminds us that Scripture is not just a set of rules or a historical text; it is the living Word of God, active and relevant in every aspect of our lives.

"Anchored in Truth" aims to inspire you to cultivate a deeper love for God's Word, seek His guidance in all things, and live out the truths found in these verses. As you read, may you be encouraged to stand firm in the faith, anchored in the unshakable truths of God's Word, and experience the wisdom, peace, and joy that come from living in alignment with His eternal commands.